MR. GILLIE and the THUNDERSTORMS

AuthorHouse™
1663 Liberty Drive
Bloomington, IN 47403
www.authorhouse.com
Phone: 1 (800) 839-8640

Published by AuthorHouse 02/21/2019

ISBN: 978-1-7283-0160-0 (sc)
ISBN: 978-1-7283-0159-4 (e)

Library of Congress Control Number: 2019902054

Print information available on the last page.

Any people depicted in stock imagery provided by Getty Images are models,
and such images are being used for illustrative purposes only.
Certain stock imagery © Getty Images.

This book is printed on acid-free paper.

MR. GILLIE and the THUNDERSTORMS

Joan Mackenzie

Well, since I have moved to Gramma's house and met some new friends, it has been lots of fun!

One day when I was sleeping, I heard a loud BANG and CRACK! I jumped up and looked out the window. Wow was it ever dark! I ran to find Max and Ruby to ask what was going on.

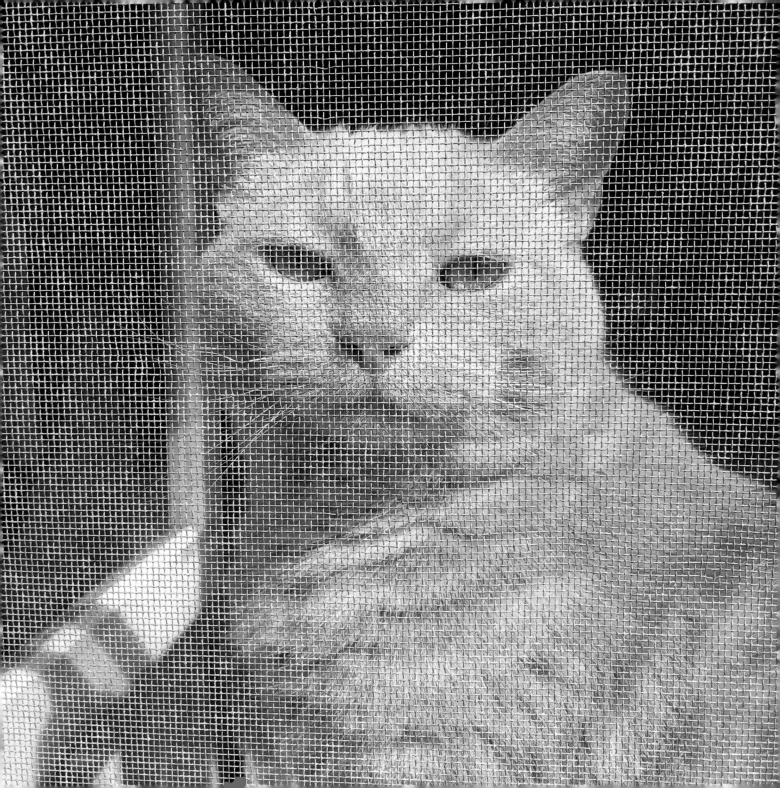

They laughed at me, "It's only a thunderstorm," they said.

"Are we ok?"

Max and Ruby said, "Yes, you silly, city boy. It's loud here because we live in a small town and there is not as much noise outside like in the city."

I ran back to the window and looked out. The rains were coming down, the streams were getting bigger and bigger and faster and faster. I thought that maybe we would be washed away. The rain still kept coming, the thunder BANGED – I was scared and ran to find Gramma.

Gramma was in the kitchen, she picked me up and cuddled me. I felt so safe. I went back to my bed and fell asleep dreaming of the butterflies. In my dream I could feel the sunshine on my fur. I opened my eyes and realized that the rain had stopped, and the sun was shining.

I got up and stretched and started to wash my face when I remembered the butterflies.

My new friends!! Were they alright, or did they get washed away? I ran to the door and Gramma let me out. I ran right into the backyard.

Wow, the grass was very wet, and the butterfly bush was hanging down. I thought it was broken but the sun was shining on it and the leaves and flowers were starting to perk up.

I looked around but there were no butterflies! I sat down very sad.

"What am I going to do? My new friends were washed away!"

I sat and wondered if I would ever see them again. All of a sudden, I heard a beautiful voice. I looked up and there was the Queen of the Butterflies.

"I thought you were gone, and I would never see you again."

She said, "we all went to the big shade tree to stay dry and now the sun is back and so are we!"

I looked up and there were all my friends, I was so happy! I found my spot under the bush and curled up. All was right with the world again, and off to sleep I went as the raindrops dripped on my nose from the bush, and the sun warmed my fur.

Mr. Gillie started to dream about a trip to the city, but again... that's another story.

Printed in the United States
By Bookmasters